1. Introduction

Agents play an important role in many search markets. In the real estate market, for example, agents improve the efficiency of the search process by helping buyers and sellers locate trading partners, identify situations where there are gains from trade, and take care of the technical details of a transaction. Agents may also have an important effect on the flow of information between buyers and sellers, depending on whom the agents work for and the nature of their legal responsibilities. For instance, if an agent helps a buyer to find trading partners, it is likely that he will learn a great deal about the buyer's preferences. Unless the agent is bound by a duty of confidentiality, he may reveal what he knows to sellers, who would presumably benefit from access to this information, since they could use it when formulating their bargaining strategy. It may be in the agent's interest to strengthen the seller's hand if, as is common in the real estate market, his compensation is proportional to the sales price that the buyer and seller negotiate.

In this paper we investigate how the role that agents play in a search market affects welfare. Our principal question is whether agents should be able to transmit information about buyers' willingness-to-pay to sellers, assuming that society's goal is to maximize the discounted expected gains from trade that the market generates. To this end, we analyze the equilibrium that arises in a search market under alternative assumptions about the agents' role. For concreteness, we develop our results using a model of the real estate market, but our conclusions are applicable to any search market in which sellers wish to sell and buyers wish to buy one unit of an indivisible good, buyers are privately informed about their valuations, and sellers' valuations are commonly known.

In our analysis, we contrast a seller's agency regime with a buyer's agency regime. These are the alternative legal regimes that have prevailed in the real estate market in recent years.[1] In the traditional seller's agency system, which was the dominant legal regime in the real estate market

_____

[1] For a thorough description of these agency relationships, see Curran and Schrag (2000), and especially Lefcoe (1993).

1

until relatively recently, all agents represent sellers' interests. Under this system, an agent in a transaction has an obligation to share with the seller any information that the buyer has revealed to the agent. In recent years it has become much more common for buyers to employ a buyer's agent in their search for a house, rather than a traditional seller's agent. Under buyer's agency, the buyer's agent works to advance the buyer's interests, and he is therefore prohibited from revealing information about his client to sellers.

After establishing that there exists an equilibrium of our theoretical model, we use a pair of numerical examples to show that it is not possible to conclude that either of the two agency regimes is generally superior, in the sense of always delivering greater total discounted expected gains from trade to a representative buyer and seller. Welfare can be higher under either agency regime. Nevertheless, we do prove a general result that identifies circumstances in which it is possible to rank the different agency regimes. Suppose that buyer's agents are at least as effective as seller's agents at introducing buyers to potential trading partners. Then a sufficient (though not necessary) condition for the buyer's agency regime to be superior to the seller's agency regime is that the time traders expect to spend in the market before reaching a deal is lower under buyer's agency than under seller's agency. Equivalently, a necessary (though not sufficient) condition for the seller's agency regime to be superior to the buyer's agency regime is that the time that traders expect to spend in the market before reaching a deal is lower under seller's agency than under buyer's agency.

These findings are reminiscent of results in the literature on the welfare effects of third-degree price discrimination by a monopolist. See, e.g., Schmalensee (1981) and Varian (1985). In this literature, third-degree price discrimination has a positive effect on social welfare (defined as the sum of producer and consumer surplus) only if it leads the monopolist to produce more units. Equivalently, the elimination of third-degree price discrimination must have a positive effect on social welfare if it is accompanied by an increase in output. The intuition behind these results is straightforward. Price discrimination may lead to an improvement in welfare if it leads a seller to sell more units and thus reduces the loss from the monopoly restriction on output. But, because a shift to price discrimination tends to cause the price of the relevant good to fall for low-valuation buyers and to rise for high-valuation buyers, units are shifted from high-valuation to low-valuation buyers, creating a misallocation of units. Thus, a necessary condition for price discrimination to be welfare improving is that it is accompanied by an output increase that can offset the negative effect of any misallocation of units. Equivalently, a sufficient condition for price discrimination to be welfare harming is that it is accompanied by an output reduction.

In our model, a seller's agency regime allows sellers to acquire information that they can use to discriminate between buyers with different valuations, and hence it is like a market in which price discrimination is possible. Of course, sellers must have some bargaining power in their meetings with buyers in order to exploit this information; for simplicity we assume that sellers make take-it-or-leave-it offers. In our model, the probability that traders conclude a deal in any meeting (which is inversely related to the time that traders expect to spend in the market) is analogous to the monopolist's output. Just as a monopolist inefficiently restricts output, sellers have a tendency to bargain with an inefficiently large number of buyers before concluding a deal. Therefore, the discounted expected gains from trade generated by the market tend to increase if the traders on average reach deals faster.

On the other hand, a seller's agency regime may lead to a misallocation of units, as occurs under third-degree price discrimination, because a well-informed seller chooses a reservation price that is correlated with her estimate of a buyer's true valuation. This pricing behavior has a tendency to reduce the likelihood that a high valuation buyer will purchase a particular house. Therefore, even if traders conclude deals faster under seller's agency, welfare may still be lower compared to buyer's agency because of the potential misallocation of properties.

These theoretical findings enable us to interpret recent empirical findings on the effect of the recent shift in the real estate market from a seller's agency regime to a buyer's agency regime. The results that Schrag and Curran (2000) and Elder, Zumpano, and Baryla (1999) present all support a conclusion that traders conclude deals faster under buyer's agency than under seller's agency. Interpreted through the lens of our theoretical results, these findings are consistent with a conclusion that welfare is higher under a buyer's agency regime than under a seller's agency regime.

Our paper contributes to the literature on search models of the real estate market by analyzing the role of agents who facilitate trades between buyers and sellers. See, for instance, Wheaton (1990) and Yavas (1992). Other papers that investigate the matchmaking role that intermediaries play in search markets include Yavas (1995), who studies whether agents can help traders avoid coordination failures, Salant (1991), who studies a seller's decision about whether or not to use an agent to sell a house, and Rubinstein and Wolinsky (1987), who analyze the factors that determine the extent to which intermediated trade replaces search by the traders themselves. None of these papers consider how the institutions that govern the relationship between intermediaries and traders affect the equilibrium that arises in search markets. This issue is our main focus. Our paper also contributes to the literature on bargaining and markets (e.g. Binmore and Herrero (1988), Samuelson (1992), and Rubinstein and Wolinsky (1990) by showing how institutions that influence the outcome of bilateral bargaining, such as agency law, have an important effect on the equilibrium of search markets.

2. A Model of the Real Estate Market

We begin by developing a model of the real estate market. Suppose that, in every period $t \in \{0, 1, 2, ...\}$, agents introduce prospective buyers to prospective sellers. We assume that there is a continuum of ex ante identical buyers and a continuum of ex ante identical sellers. For simplicity, we assume that the number of traders is the same on both sides of the market. Furthermore, we assume that, for any given buyer or seller, the probability of being matched in any given period is $q_x \in (0, 1]$, $x \in \{BA$ [Buyer's Agency], SA [Seller's Agency]$\}$. We will have

$q_{SA} \neq q_{BA}$ if the ability of agents to match buyers and sellers is different under the alternative agency relationships. Suppose, for instance, that buyers are more inclined to reveal information about their preferences under buyer's agency, when their agents are required to keep this information confidential. Or, as Elder, Zumpano, and Baryla (1999) argue, suppose that a buyer's agent has higher-powered incentives to find houses for his clients. Then we would expect to observe $q_{BA} \geq q_{SA}$, i.e. the agent would be a more effective matchmaker under buyer's agency.

Each buyer wishes to purchase one house, and each seller wishes to sell one house. In each match between a buyer and a seller, the buyer's valuation of the seller's house is a random variable, and different buyers' valuations for a given seller's house are independently and identically distributed. Define $v_t \in V = [0, \overline{v}]$ as a representative buyer's valuation of a seller's house in a match that occurs in period t.

It is reasonable to assume that a buyer is privately informed about his valuation for a particular seller's house.[2] Depending on the nature of the prevailing agency regime, however, a seller may receive information about a buyer's valuation for her house. In a seller's agency regime, a buyer's real estate agent transmits information about his valuation for a particular house to the appropriate seller. In order to model this flow of information, we suppose that, under seller's agency, the seller observes a signal $\sigma_t \in \Sigma = [\underline{\sigma}, \overline{\sigma}]$ of the buyer's valuation in period t. In a buyer's agency regime, a buyer's real estate agent does not share information about his or her client, and the seller cannot observe the realization of σ_t.

The buyer's period t valuation v_t and signal σ_t are jointly distributed according to the probability density function $f(v_t, \sigma_t)$. We assume that $f(\times, \times)$ is continuous and has full support on the domain $V \times \Sigma$. Each valuation and signal pair is independently and identically distributed. In order to reflect the idea that the seller's signal is informative about the buyer's valuation, we

---

[2] For expositional clarity, we use the feminine pronoun to refer to sellers and the masculine pronoun to refer to buyers.

assume that $f(x,x)$ satisfies the familiar monotone likelihood ratio property. Under this assumption, a higher realization of σ_t shifts the seller's posterior beliefs towards higher valuations. Formally, for $v' > v''$, $f(v', \sigma')/f(v'', \sigma') > f(v', \sigma'')/f(v'', \sigma'')$ if and only if $\sigma' > \sigma''$.

In order to simplify the model, we assume that sellers make take-it-or-leave-it offers that buyers either accept or reject.[3] Therefore, each seller chooses a pricing rule that identifies the price that she demands as a function of what, if anything, she knows about the potential buyers she could meet. Each buyer, meanwhile, chooses the acceptance rule that identifies which proposed transactions he will accept. In each match, trade occurs—and the traders exit the market—if the buyer accepts the seller's proposed price. If, in a particular match, the buyer rejects the seller's proposed price, the buyer and the seller part company and reenter the matching process in the next period. Both buyers and sellers discount future payoffs according to the common discount factor $\delta \in [0, 1)$.

The number of participants in the market fluctuates from period to period unless the entry of new buyers and sellers in each period exactly offsets the exit of traders who concluded deals in the previous period. Because the number of traders in the market may influence the probability of being matched, our assumption that q_x is constant may be strong. We do not formally model the entry of new traders into the market, but our assumption that q_x is constant could be interpreted as meaning that buyers and sellers believe that the market is in a steady-state equilibrium and that the expected number of traders does not fluctuate from period to period. Then q_x represents the buyers' and sellers' beliefs about the probability of being matched in each period under the different agency regimes.

---

[3] In an earlier version of this paper, we analyze a strategic bargaining model in which sellers and potential buyers make alternating offers. Permitting this possibility did not change our main conclusions, because privately informed buyers did not signal their information in equilibrium. Intuitively, high valuation buyers always had an incentive to deviate to some offer made by lower valuation buyers in order to elicit a favorable counteroffer from the seller. In the present model, the sellers' offers can be interpreted as counteroffers to buyers' initial (uninformative) offers.

Define the conditional probability density and distribution functions $f(v|\sigma) = \dfrac{f(v,\sigma)}{\int_0^{\bar{v}} f(x,\sigma)dx}$

and $F(v|\sigma) = \int_0^v f(x|\sigma)dx$. In the following proposition we establish that there exists a symmetric

Nash equilibrium under both buyer's agency and seller's agency if the respective hazard

functions $\dfrac{\int_x^{\bar{\sigma}} \int_x^{\bar{v}} f(z,y)dydz}{\int_{\underline{\sigma}}^{\bar{\sigma}} f(x,y)dy}$ and $\dfrac{1-F(x|\sigma)}{f(x|\sigma)}$ are decreasing in x. These assumptions are

sufficient to guarantee that a seller's expected revenue is a strictly quasi-concave function of her

reservation price and therefore has a unique maximum. We focus on symmetric equilibria in

which each (ex ante identical) seller chooses the same pricing strategy and each (ex ante

identical) buyer chooses the same offer acceptance strategy.

PROPOSITION 1: Suppose that $\dfrac{\int_{\underline{\sigma}}^{\bar{\sigma}} \int_x^{\bar{v}} f(z,y)dzdy}{\int_{\underline{\sigma}}^{\bar{\sigma}} f(x,y)dy}$ and $\dfrac{1-F(x|\sigma)}{f(x|\sigma)}$ are decreasing in x. Then

there exists a symmetric Nash equilibrium under both agency regimes.

The proofs of all results are located in Appendix 1.

In general, the symmetric Nash equilibria that arise under the two agency regimes are not

socially efficient, in the sense of maximizing the total discounted expected gains from trade that a

representative buyer and seller receive. We establish this result in the following proposition.

PROPOSITION 2: The symmetric Nash equilibria that arise under the alternative agency

relationships do not maximize the total discounted expected gains from trade in the

market. Under buyer's agency, traders expect to spend more time in the market than is

socially optimal.

The intuition for the result in Proposition 2 is straightforward. When sellers and buyers decide whether or not to conclude a deal, they do not consider the effect of their decisions on their bargaining partners. So, for instance, when a seller considers whether to reduce her reservation price and propose a deal that would be acceptable to a lower valuation buyer, she must weigh the increased probability of concluding a deal against the loss of surplus from inframarginal buyers. Of course, from a social point of view this surplus is not lost; it is merely transferred from the seller to the buyer. Because the seller is concerned with a cost that is irrelevant from the point of view of aggregate gains from trade, she is, on average, too reluctant to conclude a deal in each meeting with a buyer.

The following numerical examples illustrate that it is not possible to conclude that one of the two agency regimes always delivers higher welfare. Details of the numerical examples' solutions are located in Appendix 2. Suppose that, in each meeting between a buyer and a seller, the buyer's valuation is drawn from one of two possible distributions. If the match is a "high valuation" match, the buyer's valuation is distributed on the unit interval according to the probability density function $f_H(v) = 2v$ and the associated probability distribution function $F_H(v) = v^2$. If the match is a "low valuation" match, the buyer's valuation is distributed on the unit interval according to the probability density function $f_L(v) = 2 - 2v$ and the associated probability distribution function $F_L(v) = 2v - v^2$. We assume that the probability that any given match is a "high valuation" match is 0.5. See Figure 1 for an illustration of the two probability distribution functions.[4]

— INSERT FIGURE 1 ABOUT HERE —

_____

[4] In terms of the notation of the previous section, the valuation and signal pair (v, s) is distributed according to the joint density function $f(v, s) = \begin{cases} v, & s = H \\ 1-v, & s = L \end{cases}$, $v \in [0, 1]$.

Under seller's agency, sellers can observe whether a buyer's valuation is drawn from the "high valuation" distribution $F_H(x)$ or the "low valuation" distribution $F_L(x)$. In this case, the representative seller's strategy must specify the price that she proposes as a function of her information. Thus, the seller's strategy is a pair of prices (p^H, p^L). Under buyer's agency, sellers are unable to observe the distribution from which the buyer's valuation is drawn. In this case a seller believes that the distribution of a buyer's valuation is $F(v) = 0.5F_H(v) + 0.5F_L(v) = 0.5(v^2) + 0.5(2v - v^2) = v$, $v \in [0, 1]$, i.e. the seller believes that the buyer's valuation is distributed uniformly on the unit interval. The representative seller's strategy must now specify a price, say p^*, which she proposes in every meeting with the buyer.

The analytic solution to even this simple model is difficult to find and analyze. We therefore solve for the equilibrium of the model for different values of the parameters δ and q.[5] In Table 1 we describe the symmetric Nash equilibrium that arises under alternative assumptions about the information available to sellers, and in Table 2 we summarize the properties of these equilibria, in particular the expected price at which trades occur, the expected time that traders spend in the market, and the total expected discounted surplus that the representative buyer and seller together receive. This measure of welfare, which we denote $W = B + S$, is proportional to the total expected discounted surplus generated by the market, provided that the nature of the prevailing agency relationship does not influence people's decisions about whether to enter the market.

The results presented in the two tables are representative of the equilibria that arise under all of the different assumptions about the values of δ and q that we examined. Several features of the model's equilibrium are apparent. First, when all else is equal, buyers receive a higher expected payoff under buyer's agency, and sellers receive a higher expected payoff under seller's agency. The intuition for this finding is straightforward; when a seller has more information

---

[5] We use Mathematica v. 3.01 in order to solve for the equilibrium of the model.

about buyers' valuations for her property, she is better able to extract the gains from trade in bargaining. This intuition is also consistent with the results in Table 2, which indicate that, all else equal, the expected price of housing is higher under seller's agency.

Second, the results summarized in Table 2 indicate that, all else equal, the expected time that traders spend in the market will be lower under seller's agency. Put differently, the probability that a transaction will occur in any give match is higher under seller's agency. Finally, the results presented in Table 2 indicate that welfare is higher under seller's agency, in the sense that the combined value of the representative seller's and buyer's programs is larger. In this version of the model, welfare is higher under seller's agency because the expected time that traders spend in the market is shorter, compared to buyer's agency.

We now analyze a second example that incorporates different assumptions about the distribution of buyers' valuations. If the match is a "high valuation" match, the buyer's valuation is uniformly distributed on the unit interval, and the probability distribution function is $G_H(v) = v$, $v \in [0, 1]$. If the match is a "low valuation" match, with probability 0.1 the buyer's valuation is zero, and with probability 0.9 the buyer's valuation is uniformly distributed on the interval $[0, .9]$. In this case the probability distribution function is $G_L(v) = 0.1 + v$, $v \in [0, 0.9]$. We assume that the probability that any given match is a "high valuation" match is 0.5. See Figure 2 for an illustration of the two probability distribution functions.

— INSERT FIGURE 2 ABOUT HERE —

As before, we suppose that, under seller's agency, sellers can observe whether the buyers' valuations are drawn from the high-valuation or the low-valuation distribution. In Table 3 we describe the symmetric Nash equilibrium that arises under the alternative assumptions about the information available to sellers, and in Table 4 we summarize the properties of these equilibria.

The results presented in the two tables are consistent with the results obtained in the first example, with one prominent exception. In this example, welfare is higher under buyer's agency, despite the fact that, as before, traders conclude deals faster under seller's agency than under buyer's agency. Welfare can be lower under seller's agency because, when a seller can price discriminate, she proposes a higher price to high valuation buyers and a lower price to low valuation buyers, compared to a buyer's agency regime. But then the probability that a seller trades in a given match with a low valuation buyer rises, and the probability that a seller trades in a given match with a high valuation buyer falls, compared to buyer's agency. Under the distributional assumptions in this example, this "transfer" of units from high valuation to low valuation buyers reduces the aggregate gains from trade by enough to overcome the benefit of faster exit from the market under seller's agency.

The main conclusion that can be drawn from the two examples is that neither of the two agency regimes is always superior, in the sense of always generating greater surplus. Nevertheless, it is possible to identify some circumstances when we can rank the agency regimes. Define B_x as the value of the representative buyer's program and S_x as the value of the representative seller's program at the beginning of a period, before the traders find out if they will meet trading partners, under the agency regime $x \in \{BA, SA\}$. Because our model is stationary, the values of the representative buyer's and seller's programs do not depend on the time $t \in \{0, 1, 2, ...\}$. Define T_x as the expected time that each trader will spend in the market under agency regime x. Because we assume that the number of traders is the same on both sides of the market, buyers and sellers expect to spend the same amount of time in the market before concluding a deal. We have the following proposition.

PROPOSITION 3: Suppose that $q_{SA} \leq q_{BA}$. The representative traders' total expected discounted gains from trade are higher under buyer's agency than under seller's agency if the expected time that traders spend in the market is lower under buyer's agency. That is, $S_{SA} + B_{SA} < S_{BA} + B_{BA}$ if $T_{BA} < T_{SA}$. Equivalently, $S_{SA} + B_{SA} > S_{BA} + B_{BA}$ only if $T_{BA} > T_{SA}$.

The hypothesis of the proposition means that agents are at least as effective at matching buyers and sellers under buyer's agency as they are under seller's agency. This assumption is realistic because, as discussed in the introduction, buyers are likely to reveal more information to their agents under a buyer's agency regime. The proposition establishes that discounted expected gains from trade that a representative buyer and seller enjoy in this matching market are higher under a buyer's agency regime if traders on average conclude deals faster under buyer's agency. That is, a finding that buyers and sellers conclude deals faster under buyer's agency is sufficient to conclude that aggregate gains from trade are higher under buyer's agency. Equivalently, the discounted expected gains from trade are higher under the seller's agency regime only if traders on average conclude deals faster under seller's agency.[6]

There are two factors at work behind these results. First, a buyer's agency regime tends to deliver greater discounted expected gains from trade than seller's agency because it is not prone to the misallocation of units from high valuation to low valuation buyers that arises under price discrimination. Second, sellers tend to inefficiently prolong the search process by setting reservation prices that are too high, for the familiar reason that they do not want to give up gains from trade that they expect to capture from inframarginal buyers. Therefore, unless this advantage is offset by another factor, the agency regime that produces the shortest search time tends to yield the largest discounted expected gains from trade.

Together, these factors enable us to understand the sufficient and necessary conditions summarized in the Proposition. If search durations are shorter under buyer's agency, this fact is sufficient for a conclusion that welfare is higher under buyer's agency because that regime is inherently advantaged by the fact that it does not produce a misallocation of units between buyers. On the other hand, because seller's agency does lead to a misallocation of units, it is necessary for search durations to be shorter under seller's agency for that regime to be superior.

---

[6] It is important to point out that traders' search durations depend on both q_x and on their bargaining strategies. It is possible for traders to exit the market faster under seller's agency even if $q_{SA} < q_{BA}$.

Our theoretical results provide us with a framework that we can use to interpret recent empirical findings about the effects of different agency relationships. Curran and Schrag (2000) analyze the effect of a change in Georgia real estate law that took place in 1994. They argue that this legal change effectively introduced a buyer's agency regime into Georgia by mandating the disclosure of the agency relationships available to buyers and by instituting a reform of the Multiple Listing Service (MLS) information system that eliminated automatic subagency, a practice by which a buyer's real estate agent who used the MLS automatically became a subagent of the seller's listing agent. Curran and Schrag find that, after the legal change, both the average price of real estate and the average time that houses spent on the market declined. These findings are consistent with two conclusions. First, buyers are able to extract more gains from trade under buyer's agency. Second, traders concluded deals and exited the market faster under buyer's agency.

Elder, Zumpano, and Baryla (1999) use cross-section survey data to assess the impact of the different agency relationships. They conclude that real estate agents—including buyer's agents— have no independent effect on real estate prices, but they also find that real estate agents in general, and buyer's agents in particular, tend to reduce the time that traders spend in the market before concluding a deal.

Interpreting these empirical results through the prism of Proposition 3, they constitute evidence that aggregate, discounted expected gains from trade are higher under a buyer's agency regime than under a seller's agency regime. Of course, it is important not to overinterpret these results, because the data that the researchers use in these two empirical studies are not ideal.[7] Nevertheless, the combination of these empirical results and the theoretical results that we develop in this paper shed some light on a difficult question. The gains from trade that the real

---

[7] Curran and Schrag (2000) use time on the market data reported to the Multiple Listing Service, giving them a measure of how long an individual house was on the market before a sale. An obvious problem with these data is that they are biased downward; the time that a house was listed with a realtor who did not sell it is not reflected in the data. Elder, Zumpano, and Baryla, (1999) meanwhile, rely on survey data provided by buyers months after they completed their transactions.

estate market generates will never be observable, so any effort to identify the set of legal institutions that maximize aggregate gains from trade must rely on indirect evidence.

4.   Conclusions

In this paper we have analyzed how the flow of information influences the equilibrium in a particular kind of search market, in which buyers and sellers search for trading partners, meet, and either strike a deal or reenter the search process. Perhaps unsurprisingly, we found that it is not possible to conclude *a priori* that welfare is helped or harmed when sellers have access to information about buyers' valuations. But it is heartening that our results show that empirical analysis of potentially observable data can help to shed light on this issue.

While our model describes the real estate market reasonably well, certain aspects of this and other search markets are absent from our formalization. For instance, in our model we have abstracted away from the need to provide agents with incentives to overcome traditional moral hazard concerns. It may be worthwhile to investigate how agents' incentives and the resulting agency costs depend on the legal rules governing agents' relationships with traders. A finding that agency costs are always lower under buyer's agency would leave the conclusions of Proposition 3 unchanged, but the opposite finding (which seems unlikely) might change these conclusions.

Another issue is that, in many search markets, both buyers and sellers are repeat players, and they may find it advantageous to establish long-lasting relationships. While this issue is not present in the real estate market, it is certainly a factor in many retail and labor markets. Clearly, the possibility of repeated contact may influence both sellers' incentives to acquire information and buyers' incentives to permit the revelation of information about their personal characteristics. An analysis of this issue is an important future task.

While we have focused on the role that (human) agents play in the transmission of information in search markets, it is clear that information technology both reduces buyers' costs of searching for sellers and gives sellers greater opportunities to gather, process, and possible sell information about buyers. The recent debate on electronic commerce and privacy highlights the importance of a careful analysis of the welfare effects of these practices. While it may initially seem that consumers must suffer if firms can more easily collect information about buyers' preferences, this view neglects the possibility that, in equilibrium, fully informed consumers will demand compensation in return for revealing personal information. As long as consumers know what they are giving up, they will know what to demand in return.

APPENDIX 1: PROOFS OF PROPOSITIONS

Proof of Proposition 1: We will argue for the seller's agency case. We must show that there exists an acceptance rule for a representative buyer and a pricing rule $p(\sigma)$ for a representative seller that are mutual best replies. Consider first the representative buyer's problem. Define B as the value of the buyer's program at the beginning of a period, before he knows if he will meet a trading partner in that period. In a stationary Nash equilibrium the value of the buyer's program does not depend on time. The buyer's best reply is to purchase a house in period t if and only if $v_t - p_t \geq \delta B$, where v_t is the buyer's valuation of the house he sees in period t and p_t is the price the seller demands. If sellers choose the pricing rule $p(\sigma)$ in every period, then the value of the buyer's program is:

$$
\begin{aligned}
B &= \sum_{t=0}^{\infty} q_{SA} \int_{\underline{\sigma}}^{\overline{\sigma}} \int_{p(y)+\delta B}^{\overline{v}} (x - p(y)) f(x,y) dx dy \times \delta^t \left(1 - q_{SA} + q_{SA} \int_{\underline{\sigma}}^{\overline{\sigma}} \int_{0}^{p(y)+\delta B} f(x,y) dx dy\right)^t \\
&= \frac{q_{SA} \int_{\underline{\sigma}}^{\overline{\sigma}} \int_{p(y)+\delta B}^{\overline{v}} (x - p(y)) f(x,y) dx dy}{1 - \delta + \delta q_{SA} \int_{\underline{\sigma}}^{\overline{\sigma}} \int_{p(y)+\delta B}^{\overline{v}} f(x,y) dx dy}
\end{aligned}
$$

(1.1)

We now turn to the representative seller's problem. In each period the seller must choose a pricing rule that specifies what price she proposes as a function of the realization of her signal of the buyer's true valuation. In a stationary equilibrium the seller will choose the same pricing rule in every period.

The seller's problem is to choose a vector of pricing rules $(p_0(\sigma), p_1(\sigma), p_2(\sigma), \dots)$ to maximize the discounted expected payoff:

$$
(1.2) \quad \sum_{t=0}^{\infty} \delta^t \prod_{r=0}^{t} \left(1 - q_{SA} + q_{SA} \int_{\underline{\sigma}}^{\overline{\sigma}} \int_{0}^{p_r(y)+\delta B} f(x,y) dx dy\right) q_{SA} \int_{\underline{\sigma}}^{\overline{\sigma}} \int_{p_t(y)+\delta B}^{\overline{v}} p_t(y) f(x,y) dx dy
$$

Denoting the value of the seller's program in period t by $S(t)$, we can write the seller's problem in period t as:

$$
(1.3) \quad \max_{p_t(\cdot)} \int_{\underline{\sigma}}^{\overline{\sigma}} q_{SA} \left[\int_{p_t(y)+\delta B}^{\overline{v}} p_t(y) f(x,y) dx + \int_{0}^{p_t(y)+\delta B} \delta S(t+1) f(x,y) dx \right] dy + (1 - q_{SA}) \delta S(t+1).
$$

Appealing to standard optimal control techniques (see Takayama (1993)), the necessary condition for an interior maximum is:

$$(1.4) \quad \int_{p_t(\sigma)+\delta B}^{\bar{v}} f(x,\sigma)dx - p_t(\sigma)f(p_t(\sigma)+\delta B,\sigma) + f(p_t(\sigma)+\delta B,\sigma)\delta S(t+1) = 0, \forall \sigma \in [\underline{\sigma},\overline{\sigma}].$$

We observe that, under the hypotheses on $f(\cdot,\cdot)$, both (1.3) and (1.4) are continuous functions.

We now show that, whenever (1.4) is satisfied with equality, the second-order condition is also satisfied. Differentiating (1.4) with respect to $p_t(\sigma)$ and using (1.4) to substitute in for $p_t(\sigma)$ - δS, we have:

$$-2f(p_t(\sigma)+\delta B,\sigma) - f_1(p_t(\sigma)+\delta B,\sigma)(p_t(\sigma) - \delta S(t+1)) =$$

$$(1.5) \quad -2f(p_t(\sigma)+\delta B,\sigma) - f_1(p_t(\sigma)+\delta B,\sigma)\frac{\int_{p_t(\sigma)+\delta B}^{\bar{v}} f(z,\sigma)dz}{f(p_t(\sigma)+\delta B,\sigma)} <$$

$$-f(p_t(\sigma)+\delta B,\sigma) - f_1(p_t(\sigma)+\delta B,\sigma)\frac{\int_{p_t(\sigma)+\delta B}^{\bar{v}} f(z,\sigma)dz}{f(p_t(\sigma)+\delta B,\sigma)} < 0,$$

where the last inequality follows from the hypothesis that the hazard function is decreasing. The finding that the second order condition for a local maximum is strictly satisfied whenever (1.4) is satisfied implies that (1.3) has no interior local minima and hence is quasi-concave. But that implies that there exists a unique optimal $p_t(\sigma) \ \forall \ \sigma \in [\underline{\sigma}, \overline{\sigma}]$, and we conclude that the representative seller has a well-defined best reply. It is straightforward to show that this best-reply is always at an interior maximum; we omit the proof to save space.

It remains to show that there exist mutual best replies that form a symmetric stationary equilibrium. In such an equilibrium the value of the seller's program is:

$$(1.6) \quad S = \frac{q_{SA}\int_{\underline{\sigma}}^{\overline{\sigma}}\int_{p(y)+\delta B}^{\bar{v}} p(y)f(x,y)dxdy}{1-\delta+\delta q_{SA}\int_{\underline{\sigma}}^{\overline{\sigma}}\int_{p(y)+\delta B}^{\bar{v}} f(x,y)dxdy}.$$

Define $w(y) = p(y) + \delta B$. Adding and subtracting δB from the left-hand side of (1.4), substituting (1.6) into (1.4), using the definition of $w(y)$, and dividing by $f(w(\sigma),\sigma)$, we rewrite (1.4) as:

$$(1.7) \quad \frac{\int_{w(\sigma)}^{\bar{v}} f(x,\sigma)dx}{f(w(\sigma),\sigma)} - w(\sigma) + \frac{q_{SA}\int_{\underline{\sigma}}^{\bar{\sigma}}\int_{w(y)}^{\bar{v}} xf(x,y)dxdy}{1-\delta+\delta q_{SA}\int_{\underline{\sigma}}^{\bar{\sigma}}\int_{w(y)}^{\bar{v}} f(x,y)dxdy} = 0, \forall\sigma\in[\underline{\sigma},\bar{\sigma}].\,.$$

It remains to show that there exists a function $w(\sigma)$ that satisfies (1.7) for all σ. Define $\hat{w}(\sigma, k)$ as the function that is implicitly defined by:

$$(1.8) \quad \frac{\int_{\hat{w}}^{\bar{v}} f(x,\sigma)dx}{f(\hat{w},\sigma)} - \hat{w} + k = 0, k\in[0,\bar{v}].$$

Clearly $\hat{w}(\sigma, k)$ is a continuous function, and well-known results about the monotone likelihood ratio property guarantee that it is an increasing function of σ. Define the function:

$$(1.9) \quad W(k) = \frac{q_{SA}\int_{\underline{\sigma}}^{\bar{\sigma}}\int_{\hat{w}(y,k)}^{\bar{v}} xf(x,y)dxdy}{1-\delta+\delta q_{SA}\int_{\underline{\sigma}}^{\bar{\sigma}}\int_{\hat{w}(y,k)}^{\bar{v}} f(x,y)dxdy}.$$

Recognizing that $W: [0, \bar{v}] \to [0, \bar{v}]$ and that $W(\cdot)$ is continuous, Brouwer's fixed point theorem establishes that $\exists\, k^* \in [0, \bar{v}]$ such that $W(k^*) = k^*$. Define $w^*(\sigma) = \hat{w}(\sigma, k^*)$. By construction $w^*(\sigma)$ satisfies (1.7) for all $\sigma \in \Sigma = [\underline{\sigma}, \bar{\sigma}]$. Using the definitions of $w^*(\sigma)$ and B, it is possible to recover B and $p(\sigma)$, which in turn define the representative buyer's and seller's mutual best replies and the resulting symmetric Nash equilibrium.

Similar arguments establish the existence of a symmetric Nash equilibrium in the buyer's agency case.

QED

Proof of Proposition 2: Define ω_t as the valuation of the marginal buyer in period t. To maximize the aggregate discounted expected gains from trade, choose $(\omega_0, \omega_1, \omega_2,...)$ in order to maximize:

$$(2.1) \quad \sum_{t=0}^{\infty}\delta^t\prod_{r=0}^{t}(1-q\int_{\underline{\sigma}}^{\bar{\sigma}}\int_{\omega_r}^{\bar{v}} f(x,y)dxdy)q\int_{\underline{\sigma}}^{\bar{\sigma}}\int_{\omega_r}^{\bar{v}} x\times f(x,y)dxdy$$

where $q \in \{q_{SA}, q_{BA}\}$ is the probability of being matched in a period. It is straightforward to differentiate (2.1) and establish that maximizing (2.1) involves choosing the same marginal buyer "cutoff" in every period. Writing the aggregate gains from trade W as a function of the cutoff, say ω, the problem is:

$$(2.2) \qquad \max_{\omega \in [0, \bar{v}]} W = \frac{q \int_{\underline{\sigma}}^{\bar{\sigma}} \int_{\omega}^{\bar{v}} x \times f(x, y) dx dy}{1 - \delta + \delta q \int_{\underline{\sigma}}^{\bar{\sigma}} \int_{\omega}^{\bar{v}} f(x, y) dx dy} .$$

The necessary condition for an interior maximum is:

$$(2.3) \qquad \frac{dW}{d\omega} = \frac{q \int_{\underline{\sigma}}^{\bar{\sigma}} f(\omega^*, y) dy \left[-\omega^* + \dfrac{\delta q \int_{\underline{\sigma}}^{\bar{\sigma}} \int_{\omega^*}^{\bar{v}} x f(x, y) dx dy}{(1 - \delta + \delta q \int_{\underline{\sigma}}^{\bar{\sigma}} \int_{\omega^*}^{\bar{v}} f(x, y) dx dy)} \right]}{(1 - \delta + \delta q \int_{\underline{\sigma}}^{\bar{\sigma}} \int_{\omega^*}^{\bar{v}} f(x, y) dx dy)} = 0 .$$

Define ω^* as the value of ω that satisfies (2.3). Differentiating (2.3), evaluating the result at ω^*, and using (2.3), we have:

$$(2.4) \qquad \frac{d^2 W}{d\omega^2} = \frac{- \int_{\underline{\sigma}}^{\bar{\sigma}} f(\omega^*, y) dy}{1 - \delta + \delta q \int_{\underline{\sigma}}^{\bar{\sigma}} \int_{\omega^*}^{\bar{v}} f(x, y) dx dy} < 0 .$$

Thus, the second order condition is satisfied whenever (2.3) is satisfied, implying that $W(\omega)$ has no interior minimum and hence is quasiconcave and has a unique maximum. It is straightforward to show that $\omega^* < \bar{v}$. Furthermore, $W'(\omega) < 0$ for all $\omega > \omega^*$, and $W' > 0$ for all $\omega < \omega^*$.

We now consider the buyer's agency case. Arguments analogous to those in the proof of Proposition 1 establish that, in equilibrium, the valuation of the marginal buyer in each period, say ω_{BA}^*, satisfies

$$(2.5) \quad \frac{\int_{\omega_{BA}^*}^{\bar{v}} f(x,\sigma)dx}{f(\omega_{BA}^*,\sigma)} - \omega_{BA}^* + \frac{q_{BA}\int_{\underline{\sigma}}^{\bar{\sigma}}\int_{\omega_{BA}^*}^{\bar{v}} xf(x,y)dxdy}{1-\delta+\delta q_{BA}\int_{\underline{\sigma}}^{\bar{\sigma}}\int_{\omega_{BA}^*}^{\bar{v}} f(x,y)dxdy} = 0$$

Because the hazard function is non-negative, we must have:

$$(2.6) \quad -\omega_{BA}^* + \frac{q_{BA}\int_{\underline{\sigma}}^{\bar{\sigma}}\int_{\omega_{BA}^*}^{\bar{v}} xf(x,y)dxdy}{1-\delta+\delta q_{BA}\int_{\underline{\sigma}}^{\bar{\sigma}}\int_{\omega_{BA}^*}^{\bar{v}} f(x,y)dxdy} < 0$$

Comparing (2.6) to (2.3) and using quasiconcavity of $W(\omega)$, it immediately follows that $\omega_{BA}^* > \omega^*$, establishing that the probability of trade is lower in any given meeting under buyer's agency than if the marginal buyer's valuation were ω^*. Therefore, traders expect to spend more time than is optimal in the market under buyer's agency. *A fortiori* the Nash equilibrium under buyer's agency does not maximize the aggregate discounted expected gains from trade.

Similar arguments establish that the Nash equilibrium under seller's agency does not maximize the aggregate discounted expected gains from trade; we omit the proof to save space.

QED

Proof of Proposition 3: Define $\omega_{SA}(\sigma) = p_{SA}(\sigma) + \delta B_{SA}$, where $p_{SA}(\sigma)$ is the seller's equilibrium pricing rule under a seller's agency regime. Define $\omega_{BA} = p_{BA} + \delta B_{BA}$, where p_{BA} is the seller's equilibrium price under a buyer's agency regime. It is straightforward to calculate that $T_x = \dfrac{1}{q_x \int_{\underline{\sigma}}^{\bar{\sigma}}\int_{\omega_x(y)}^{\bar{v}} f(x,y)dxdy}$, $x \in \{BA, SA\}$. We must show that

$$S_{SA} + B_{SA} = \frac{q_{SA}\int_{\underline{\sigma}}^{\bar{\sigma}}\int_{\omega_{SA}(y)}^{\bar{v}} x\times f(x,y)dxdy}{1-\delta+\delta q_{SA}\int_{\underline{\sigma}}^{\bar{\sigma}}\int_{\omega_{SA}(y)}^{\bar{v}} f(x,y)dxdy} > S_{BA} + B_{BA} = \frac{q_{BA}\int_{\underline{\sigma}}^{\bar{\sigma}}\int_{\omega_{BA}}^{\bar{v}} x\times f(x,y)dxdy}{1-\delta+\delta q_{BA}\int_{\underline{\sigma}}^{\bar{\sigma}}\int_{\omega_{BA}}^{\bar{v}} f(x,y)dxdy}$$

only if $q_{SA}\int_{\underline{\sigma}}^{\bar{\sigma}}\int_{\omega_{SA}(y)}^{\bar{v}} f(x,y)dxdy > q_{BA}\int_{\underline{\sigma}}^{\bar{\sigma}}\int_{\omega_{BA}}^{\bar{v}} f(x,y)dxdy$.

Suppose to the contrary that $q_{SA} \int_{\underline{\sigma}}^{\bar{\sigma}} \int_{\omega_{SA}(y)}^{\bar{\nu}} f(x,y) dx dy < q_{BA} \int_{\underline{\sigma}}^{\bar{\sigma}} \int_{\omega_{BA}}^{\bar{\nu}} f(x,y) dx dy$ and $S_{SA} + B_{SA} >$

$S_{BA} + B_{BA}$. Define $\hat{\omega}$ as satisfying $\int_{\underline{\sigma}}^{\bar{\sigma}} \int_{\hat{\omega}}^{\bar{\nu}} f(x,y) dx dy = \int_{\underline{\sigma}}^{\bar{\sigma}} \int_{\omega_{SA}(y)}^{\bar{\nu}} f(x,y) dx dy$. Because $\omega_{SA}(\sigma)$ is

increasing (see the proof of Proposition 1), it is straightforward to establish that

$$\int_{\underline{\sigma}}^{\bar{\sigma}} \int_{\omega_{SA}(y)}^{\bar{\nu}} \frac{x \cdot f(x,y)}{\int_{\underline{\sigma}}^{\bar{\sigma}} \int_{\omega_{SA}(y)}^{\bar{\nu}} f(x,y) dx dy} dx dy < \int_{\underline{\sigma}}^{\bar{\sigma}} \int_{\hat{\omega}}^{\bar{\nu}} \frac{x \cdot f(x,y)}{\int_{\underline{\sigma}}^{\bar{\sigma}} \int_{\hat{\omega}}^{\bar{\nu}} f(x,y) dx dy} dx dy \text{, implying that}$$

$$\frac{q_{SA} \int_{\underline{\sigma}}^{\bar{\sigma}} \int_{\omega_{SA}(y)}^{\bar{\nu}} x \times f(x,y) dx dy}{1 - \delta + \delta q_{SA} \int_{\underline{\sigma}}^{\bar{\sigma}} \int_{\omega_{SA}(y)}^{\bar{\nu}} f(x,y) dx dy} < \frac{q_{SA} \int_{\underline{\sigma}}^{\bar{\sigma}} \int_{\hat{\omega}}^{\bar{\nu}} x \times f(x,y) dx dy}{1 - \delta + \delta q_{SA} \int_{\underline{\sigma}}^{\bar{\sigma}} \int_{\hat{\omega}}^{\bar{\nu}} f(x,y) dx dy} \text{. It remains only to show that}$$

$$\frac{q_{SA} \int_{\underline{\sigma}}^{\bar{\sigma}} \int_{\hat{\omega}}^{\bar{\nu}} x \times f(x,y) dx dy}{1 - \delta + \delta q_{SA} \int_{\underline{\sigma}}^{\bar{\sigma}} \int_{\hat{\omega}}^{\bar{\nu}} f(x,y) dx dy} < \frac{q_{BA} \int_{\underline{\sigma}}^{\bar{\sigma}} \int_{\omega_{BA}}^{\bar{\nu}} x \times f(x,y) dx dy}{1 - \delta + \delta q_{BA} \int_{\underline{\sigma}}^{\bar{\sigma}} \int_{\omega_{BA}}^{\bar{\nu}} f(x,y) dx dy} \text{, forcing a contradiction and}$$

establishing the result.

By hypothesis $q_{SA} \int_{\underline{\sigma}}^{\bar{\sigma}} \int_{\omega_{SA}(y)}^{\bar{\nu}} f(x,y) dx dy = q_{SA} \int_{\underline{\sigma}}^{\bar{\sigma}} \int_{\hat{\omega}}^{\bar{\nu}} f(x,y) dx dy < q_{BA} \int_{\underline{\sigma}}^{\bar{\sigma}} \int_{\omega_{BA}}^{\bar{\nu}} f(x,y) dx dy$, so

$$\frac{q_{SA} \int_{\underline{\sigma}}^{\bar{\sigma}} \int_{\hat{\omega}}^{\bar{\nu}} x \times f(x,y) dx dy}{1 - \delta + \delta q_{SA} \int_{\underline{\sigma}}^{\bar{\sigma}} \int_{\hat{\omega}}^{\bar{\nu}} f(x,y) dx dy} > \frac{q_{BA} \int_{\underline{\sigma}}^{\bar{\sigma}} \int_{\omega_{BA}}^{\bar{\nu}} x \times f(x,y) dx dy}{1 - \delta + \delta q_{BA} \int_{\underline{\sigma}}^{\bar{\sigma}} \int_{\omega_{BA}}^{\bar{\nu}} f(x,y) dx dy} \text{ only if}$$

$$\int_{\underline{\sigma}}^{\bar{\sigma}} \int_{\hat{\omega}}^{\bar{\nu}} \frac{x \cdot f(x,y)}{\int_{\underline{\sigma}}^{\bar{\sigma}} \int_{\hat{\omega}}^{\bar{\nu}} f(x,y) dx dy} dx dy > \int_{\underline{\sigma}}^{\bar{\sigma}} \int_{\omega_{BA}}^{\bar{\nu}} \frac{x \cdot f(x,y)}{\int_{\underline{\sigma}}^{\bar{\sigma}} \int_{\omega_{BA}}^{\bar{\nu}} f(x,y) dx dy} dx dy \text{, i.e. only if } \hat{\omega} > \omega_{BA}. \text{ Define } W(\omega, q)$$

$$= \frac{q \int_{\underline{\sigma}}^{\bar{\sigma}} \int_{\omega}^{\bar{\nu}} x \times f(x,y) dx dy}{1 - \delta + \delta q \int_{\underline{\sigma}}^{\bar{\sigma}} \int_{\omega}^{\bar{\nu}} f(x,y) dx dy} \text{. Differentiation establishes that } \partial W / \partial q > 0 \text{, so the hypothesis that}$$

$q_{SA} \leq q_{BA}$ implies that $W(\omega, q_{SA}) \leq W(\omega, q_{BA})$. Arguments given in the proof of Proposition 2

establish that $W(\omega, q)$ is a quasiconcave function of ω, and Proposition 2 establishes that $\omega_{BA} >$

$\text{argmax}_{\omega \in [0, \bar{v}]} W(\omega, q_{BA})$. Because $\hat{\omega} > \omega_{BA}$, we then have $W(\omega_{BA}, q_{BA}) > W(\hat{\omega}, q_{BA}) \geq W(\hat{\omega}, q_{SA})$, from which it follows that $\dfrac{q_{SA} \displaystyle\int_{\underline{\sigma}}^{\bar{\sigma}} \int_{\omega_{SA}(y)}^{\bar{v}} x \times f(x,y)\,dx\,dy}{1 - \delta + \delta q_{SA} \displaystyle\int_{\underline{\sigma}}^{\bar{\sigma}} \int_{\omega_{SA}(y)}^{\bar{v}} f(x,y)\,dx\,dy} < \dfrac{q_{BA} \displaystyle\int_{\underline{\sigma}}^{\bar{\sigma}} \int_{\omega_{BA}}^{\bar{v}} x \times f(x,y)\,dx\,dy}{1 - \delta + \delta q_{BA} \displaystyle\int_{\underline{\sigma}}^{\bar{\sigma}} \int_{\omega_{BA}}^{\bar{v}} f(x,y)\,dx\,dy}$, a

contradiction.

QED

APPENDIX 2: NUMERICAL EXAMPLES

Example 1:

We first consider the seller's agency case. The representative seller's strategy (p^H, p^L) must satisfy the following equilibrium conditions, corresponding to equation (1.4) in the proof of Proposition 1.

$$(1) \quad \frac{1-(p^H+\delta B)^2}{2(p^H+\delta B)} - p^H + \frac{\delta q(0.5\int_{p^H+\delta B}^{1}2xp^H dx + 0.5\int_{p^L+\delta B}^{1}(2-2x)p^L dx)}{1-\delta+\delta q(0.5(1-(p^H+\delta B)^2)+0.5(1-2(p^L+\delta B)+(p^L+\delta B)^2))} = 0$$

$$(2) \quad \frac{1-2(p^L+\delta B)+(p^L+\delta B)^2}{2-2(p^L+\delta B)} - p^L + $$
$$\frac{\delta q(0.5\int_{p^H+\delta B}^{1}2xp^H dx + 0.5\int_{p^L+\delta B}^{1}(2-2x)p^L dx)}{1-\delta+\delta q(0.5(1-(p^H+\delta B)^2)+0.5(1-2(p^L+\delta B)+(p^L+\delta B)^2))} = 0$$

Meanwhile, the value of the representative buyer's program is given by:

$$(3) \quad B = \frac{\delta q(0.5\int_{p^H+\delta B}^{1}2x(x-p^H)dx + 0.5\int_{p^L+\delta B}^{1}(2-2x)(x-p^L dx)}{1-\delta+\delta q(0.5(1-(p^H+\delta B)^2)+0.5(1-2(p^L+\delta B)+(p^L+\delta B)^2))} = 0.$$

In order to solve for an equilibrium, it is helpful to define the variables $w^H = p^H + \delta B$ and $w^L = p^L + \delta B$. Adding and subtracting δB to the left-hand side of (1) and (2) and using the definition of B, we have the following equilibrium conditions.

$$(4) \quad \frac{1-(w^H)^2}{2w^H} - w^H + \frac{\delta q(0.5\int_{w^H}^{1}2x^2 dx + 0.5\int_{w^L}^{1}(2-2x)x dx)}{1-\delta+\delta q(0.5(1-(w^H)^2)+0.5(1-2w^L+(w^L)^2))} = 0$$

$$(5) \quad \frac{1-2w^L+(w^L)^2}{2-2w^L} - w^L + \frac{\delta q(0.5\int_{w^H}^{1}2x^2 dx + 0.5\int_{w^L}^{1}(2-2x)x dx)}{1-\delta+\delta q(0.5(1-(w^H)^2)+0.5(1-2w^L+(w^L)^2))} = 0$$

Equations (4) and (5) represent a system of two equations in two unknowns, w^H and w^L. In principle, it is possible to solve this system of equations and then use the definitions of B, w^H, and w^L to solve for B, p^H, and p^L.

We now consider the buyer's agency case. The seller's strategy p^* must satisfy the following equilibrium condition, which is analogous to equations (1) and (2).

$$(6) \qquad 1-(p^*+\delta B)-p^*+\frac{\delta q \int_{p^*+\delta B}^{1} p \, dx}{1-\delta+\delta q(1-p^*-\delta B)}=0$$

Meanwhile, the value of the representative buyer's program is given by:

$$(7) \qquad B=\frac{q\int_{p^*+\delta B}^{1}(x-p^*)dx}{1-\delta+\delta q(1-p^*-\delta B)}.$$

In order to solve for an equilibrium, it is helpful to define the variable $w^* = p^* + \delta B$. Adding and subtracting δB to the left-hand side of (6) and using the definition of B, we have the following equilibrium condition.

$$(8) \qquad 1-2w^*+\frac{\delta q \int_{w^*}^{1} x \, dx}{1-\delta+\delta q(1-w^*)}=0$$

In principle, it is possible to solve equation (8) for w^* and then use the definitions of B and w^* to solve for B and p.

Example 2:

We first consider the seller's agency case. Assuming that the seller trades with positive probability in every match with a buyer, meaning that $p^L \le 0.9$, the representative seller's strategy must satisfy the following equilibrium conditions.

$$(9) \qquad 1-(p^H+\delta B)-p^H+\frac{\delta q(0.5\int_{p^H+\delta B}^{1} p^H dx+0.5\int_{p^L+\delta B}^{.9} p^L dx)}{1-\delta+\delta q(0.5(1-p^H-\delta B)+0.5(.9-p^L-\delta B))}=0$$

$$(10) \qquad .9-(p^L+\delta B)-p^L+\frac{\delta q(0.5\int_{p^H+\delta B}^{1} p^H dx+0.5\int_{p^L+\delta B}^{.9} p^L dx)}{1-\delta+\delta q(0.5(1-p^H-\delta B)+0.5(.9-p^L-\delta B))}=0.$$

Meanwhile, the value of the representative buyer's program is given by:

$$(11) \qquad B = \frac{q(0.5\int_{p^H+\delta B}^{1}(x-p^H)dx + 0.5\int_{p^L+\delta B}^{.9}(x-p^L)dx)}{1-\delta+\delta q(0.5(1-p^H-\delta B)+0.5(.9-p^L-\delta B))}.$$

It is helpful to define the variables $w^H = p^H + \delta B$ and $w^L = p^L + \delta B$. Adding and subtracting δB to the left-hand side of (9) and (10) and using the definition of B, we have the following equilibrium conditions.

$$(12) \qquad 1-2w^H + \frac{\delta q(0.5\int_{w^H}^{1} x dx + 0.5\int_{w^L}^{.9} x dx)}{1-\delta+\delta q(0.5(1-w^H)+0.5(.9-w^L))} = 0$$

$$(13) \qquad .9-2w^L + \frac{\delta q(0.5\int_{w^H}^{1} x dx + 0.5\int_{w^L}^{.9} x dx)}{1-\delta+\delta q(0.5(1-w^H)+0.5(.9-w^L))} = 0$$

Equations (12) and (13) represent a system of two equations in two unknowns, w^H and w^L. In principle, it is possible to solve this system of equations and then use the definitions of B, w^H, and w^L to solve for B, p^H, and p^L.

We now consider the buyer's agency case. Assuming that the seller trades with positive probability in every match, i.e. that $p < 0.9$, the seller's strategy $p*$ must satisfy the following equilibrium condition.

$$(14) \qquad .95-(p*+\delta B)-p* + \frac{\delta q(0.5\int_{p*+\delta B}^{1} p dx + 0.5\int_{p*+\delta B}^{.9} p dx)}{1-\delta+\delta q(0.5(1-p*-\delta B)+0.5(.9-p*-\delta B))} = 0$$

Meanwhile, the value of the representative buyer's program is given by:

$$(15) \qquad B = \frac{q(0.5\int_{p*+\delta B}^{1}(x-p*)dx + 0.5\int_{p*+\delta B}^{.9}(x-p*)dx)}{1-\delta+\delta q(0.5(1-p*-\delta B)+0.5(.9-p*-\delta B))}.$$

In order to solve for an equilibrium, it is helpful to define the variable $w* = p* + \delta B$. Adding and subtracting δB to the left-hand side of (14) and using the definition of B, we have the following equilibrium condition.

$$(16) \quad .95 - 2w* + \frac{\delta q(0.5 \int_{w*}^{1} xdx + 0.5 \int_{w*}^{.9} xdx)}{1 - \delta + \delta q(0.5(1 - w*) + 0.5(.9 - w*))} = 0$$

In principle, it is possible to solve equation (16) for $w*$ and then use the definitions of B and $w*$ to solve for B and $p*$.

		Seller's Agency	**Buyer's Agency**
$\delta = .9, q = 1$	Seller's Strategy	$p^H = .6601, p^L = .5793$	$p* = .6444$
	Seller's Expected Payoff	.4903	.4849
	Buyer's Expected Payoff	.1608	.1640
$\delta = .9, q = .75$	Seller's Strategy	$p^H = .6482, p^L = .5570$	$p* = .6295$
	Seller's Expected Payoff	.4489	.4432
	Buyer's Expected Payoff	.1523	.1554
$\delta = .95, q = 1$	Seller's Strategy	$p^H = .6642, p^L = .6061$	$p* = .6544$
	Seller's Expected Payoff	.5294	.5252
	Buyer's Expected Payoff	.1972	.2001
$\delta = .95, q = .75$	Seller's Strategy	$p^H = .6540, p^L = .5878$	$p* = .6421$
	Seller's Expected Payoff	.4968	.4922
	Buyer's Expected Payoff	.1899	.1930

TABLE 1: NASH EQUILIBRIUM IN EXAMPLE ONE

		Seller's Agency	Buyer's Agency
$\delta = .9, q = 1$	Expected Price ($\bar{P}*$)	.6457	.6444
	Expected Time in Market ($\bar{T}*$)	4.67	4.81
	Welfare ($B + S$)	.6511	.6489
$\delta = .9, q = .75$	Expected Price ($\bar{P}*$)	.6303	.6295
	Expected Time in Market ($\bar{T}*$)	5.59	5.78
	Welfare ($B + S$)	.6012	.5985
$\delta = .95, q = 1$	Expected Price ($\bar{P}*$)	.6564	.6544
	Expected Time in Market ($\bar{T}*$)	6.30	6.43
	Welfare ($B + S$)	.7265	.7253
$\delta = .95, q = .75$	Expected Price ($\bar{P}*$)	.6440	.6421
	Expected Time in Market ($\bar{T}*$)	7.46	7.64
	Welfare ($B + S$)	.6867	.6852

TABLE 2: NUMERICAL RESULTS FROM EXAMPLE ONE

		Seller's Agency	**Buyer's Agency**
$\delta = .9, q = 1$	Seller's Strategy	$p^H = .5916, p^L = .5416$	$p* = .5592$
	Seller's Expected Payoff	.4071	.3999
	Buyer's Expected Payoff	.2035	.2122
$\delta = .9, q = .75$	Seller's Strategy	$p^H = .5843, p^L = .5343$	$p* = .5538$
	Seller's Expected Payoff	.3747	.3689
	Buyer's Expected Payoff	.1873	.1938
$\delta = .95, q = 1$	Seller's Strategy	$p^H = .6086, p^L = .5586$	$p* = .5680$
	Seller's Expected Payoff	.4573	.4415
	Buyer's Expected Payoff	.2287	.2457
$\delta = .95, q = .75$	Seller's Strategy	$p^H = .6024, p^L = .5524$	$p* = .5657$
	Seller's Expected Payoff	.4313	.4195
	Buyer's Expected Payoff	.2156	.2285

TABLE 3: NASH EQUILIBRIUM IN EXAMPLE TWO

		Seller's Agency	Buyer's Agency
$\delta = .9, q = 1$	Expected Price ($\overline{P}*$)	.5697	.5592
	Expected Time in Market ($\overline{T}*$)	4.99	5.00
	Welfare ($B + S$)	.6106	.6115
$\delta = .9, q = .75$	Expected Price ($\overline{P}*$)	.5621	.5538
	Expected Time in Market ($\overline{T}*$)	6.00	6.01
	Welfare ($B + S$)	.5620	.5627
$\delta = .95, q = 1$	Expected Price ($\overline{P}*$)	.5878	.5680
	Expected Time in Market ($\overline{T}*$)	6.71	6.73
	Welfare ($B + S$)	.6860	.6872
$\delta = .95, q = .75$	Expected Price ($\overline{P}*$)	.5812	.5657
	Expected Time in Market ($\overline{T}*$)	7.95	7.97
	Welfare ($B + S$)	.6469	.6479

TABLE 4: NUMERICAL RESULTS FROM EXAMPLE TWO

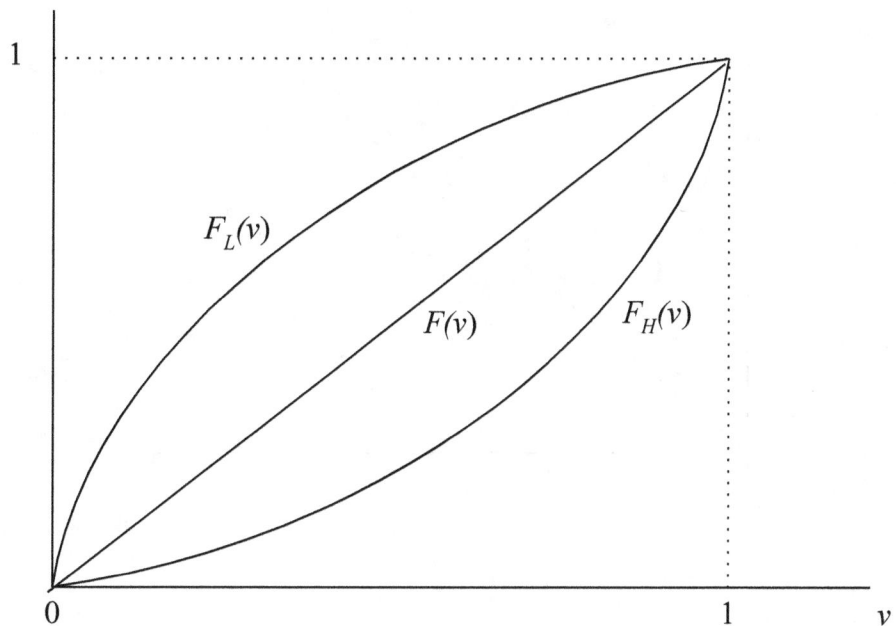

FIGURE 1: DISTRIBUTIONS IN EXAMPLE ONE

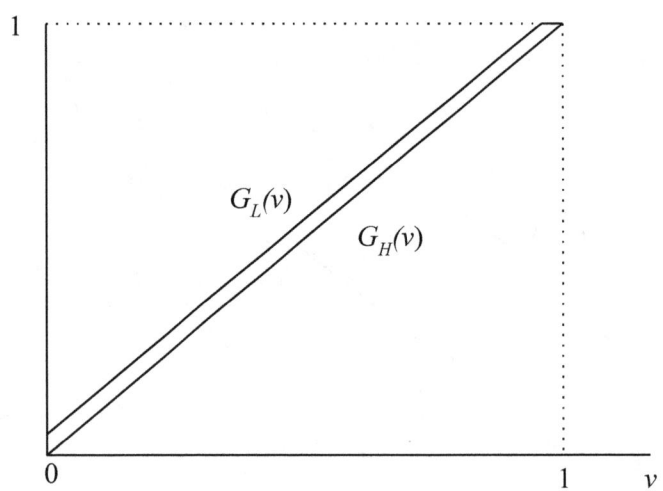

FIGURE 2: DISTRIBUTIONS IN EXAMPLE TWO

REFERENCES

Binmore, K.G. and M.J. Herrero. (1988) "Matching and Bargaining in Dynamic Markets," *Review of Economic* Studies **55**:17-31.

Curran, Christopher and Joel Schrag. (2000) "Does it Matter Whom An Agent Serves? Evidence From Recent Changes in Real Estate Agency Law," *Journal of Law and Economics* **43**: 265 – 284.

Elder, Harold and Leonard Zumpano and Edward Baryla. (1999) "Buyer Brokers: Do They Make a Difference? Their Impact on Selling Price and Search Duration." Forthcoming, *Real Estate Economics.*

Lefcoe, George. (1993) *Real Estate Transactions.* Charlottesville: Michie.

Rubinstein, Ariel and Asher Wolinsky. (1987) "Middlemen," *Quarterly Journal of Economics* **102**:581-593.

_____. (1990) "Decentralized Trading, Strategic Behaviour and the Walrasian Outcome," *Review of Economic Studies* **57**:63-78.

Salant, Stephen W. (1991) "For Sale by Owner: When to Use a Broker and How to Price the House," *Journal of Real Estate Finance and Economics* **4**:157-173.

Samuelson, Larry. (1992) "Disagreement in Markets with Matching and Bargaining." *Review of Economic Studies* **59**:177-185.

Schmalensee, Richard. (1981) "Output and Welfare Implications of Monopolistic Third-Degree Price Discrimination." *American Economic Review* **71**: 242 – 247.

Takayama, Akira. (1993) *Analytical Methods in Economics.* Ann Arbor: University of Michigan Press.

Varian, Hal. (1985) "Price Discrimination and Social Welfare." *American Economic Review* **75**: 870 – 875.

Wheaton, William C. (1990) "Vacancy, Search, and Prices in a Housing Market Matching Model, *Journal of Political Economy* **98**:1270-1292.

Yavas, Abdullah. (1992) "A Simple Search and Bargaining Model of Real Estate Markets," *AREUEA Journal* **20**:533-548.

_____. (1995) "Can Brokerage Have an Equilibrium Selection Role?" *Journal of Urban Economics* **37**:17-37.